For Eric, Florence and Andrew

Contents

The Board Room

"Well, that's it, then."

The statement was empty, flat, resigned. By this stage, eye contact around the table was nonexistent, so the chairman stared through the window and addressed the remark in the general direction of the clock tower. This impressive and still-functioning monument had kept time for the venerable institution for the past 96 years and, in doing so, had come to symbolize the coalescence of the company values of the past, the challenges of the present and its aspirations for the future. Gloomy though the future looked, the clock tower's sense of benevolence and permanence provided the chairman some solace to the gloom and resignation around the table.

This had been the most painful discussion in the most painful process he had been through. He had hoped, he told the assembled board, that his generation would not be the one to take such a drastic step and make such a final decision, but the alternative had never materialized—his son, Richard, had flinched at those words—and there was no choice.

He took comfort from the clock tower and finished his conclusion. "Well, that's it, then. We sell."

The Corner Office

So that was it, then.

The old man was holding good to his threat or, rather, his promise. Richard's father had repeatedly warned him that the generation that failed to lead well would no longer lead at all—the previous generation would see to that. His grandfather had given the same warning to Richard's father, and Richard's grandfather had received it from his father. But the first two generations had the good fortune of never having to exercise the threat. Deeply ingrained in each generation was the conviction that good companies are the product of good leadership and, if the family failed to provide good leadership, the generational mandate was to sell.

At the close of the board meeting, everyone left the conference room in silence, avoiding any eye contact with the chairman as they shuffled past him. When Richard passed by his father, he thought for a moment that his father wanted to keep him back, but thought better of it. Richard didn't want to face that conversation anyway and made the short walk to his office as quickly as he could.

He wanted to be alone to process the decision and absorb its impact as the deep sense of personal failure began to sink in. The alternative that "had never materialized," as his father had gently but truthfully stated, was the issue of Richard's effectiveness as a leader. Ever since his father had handed him the reins of the company, he had presided over a downward spiral that he had failed to halt. The exodus of key executive team members (two of them by his decision), high turn-over in the ranks immediately below, the sapping morale in the rank and file, the weakening pipeline in research and development, and the internal sentiment that the company was losing its bearings—all contributed to the final and sadly historical decision made barely 15 minutes earlier. The dismal financial performance no doubt contributed, though it was not necessarily the driving factor; this wasn't the first time finances had been weak or even alarming, but poor financial performance had always been taken in its context. In this case, it simply reinforced every non-financial metric that had led to the decision.

The pit in his stomach got a small measure of temporary relief as he paced up and down in front of the large window that looked over the historic courtyard in the center of the company's sprawling campus. As he looked in the general direction of the clock tower, the objects of his anger filed past him one after the other.

The first was his father, who had failed to give him the support he needed and had now cast him off like a piece of obsolete equipment. He ignored the nagging thought that his father may have tried and been rebuffed, and he moved on to his family. He cursed the day he was born into a generation that carried such weight from its prede-cessors. Why couldn't he have been his great-grandfather? Why was he born into this family at all? He regretted ever joining the family business, and wished he'd made the same choice his two brothers had made. As a doctor and as a teacher, they wanted nothing to do with the company. Now he had to deal with the family stigma of leading the generation that failed to retain the family business. Instead of the electrical engineering degree from Penn State and the master's from MIT, he wished he'd taken his studies in a direction not so obviously associated with the company's business. He thought with regret about the offers from Boeing and Martin Marietta he turned down, but he also reluctantly acknowledged that he might still be facing the same leadership issues, just in a different context.

The pit in his stomach tightened again as he thought about the early days. He had started out with such promise. He had transformed three departments (IT, R&D and Sales) and brought to bear his considerable project management skills to the sloppiness that existed in each one when he took it over. He had won over the skepticism of non-family members and it was clear that his appointments were no sinecure. And in the marketplace, the company's reputation as an innovator was still untarnished. The more he thought about it, the more his anger turned to the board—couldn't they recognize any of these successes? Didn't his accomplishments count for anything? Why hadn't those successes been more prominent during those painful discussions?

Taking over from his father had been an exciting move and, at 41, he had felt ready for it. Three years later, he wished he hadn't. Success back then had seemed so inevitable, failure so unimaginable. Now success was a dream and failure a reality.

He turned away from the clock tower and slumped into his chair.

So this was it, then.

The Clock Tower

"Well, that's it, then."

The mood in the clock tower wasn't much different.

Three figures, normally combative and argumentative, were uncharacteristically subdued and solemn. "Well, that's it, then. They have decided to sell."

The statement, however, wasn't made with the same sense of resignation as the chairman's. It came with quiet urgency and determination. "The time for bickering is over. We have some work to do."

The statement came from a tall man with gray hair and a slender build. His square jaw gave him a permanently firm expression, and his gray eyes, accentuated by his gray hair, gave the impression he was always looking past you to something beyond. The overall impression was not unfriendly, but it was not intimate.

The other two couldn't have been more different physically or temperamentally. One was shorter but stockier, with a strong chest and strong arms, clearly an aficionado of workout rooms. His eyes gleamed with intensity and he had the no-nonsense, down-to-earth demeanor of an ex-Marine. Not someone to mess with.

The third was big and chubby, with the look of a soft, pudgy teddy bear—definitely not an aficionado of workout rooms. His fleshy face had a captivating smile, and of the three, he was the one who communicated the most genuine interest in the people he encountered.

Deep down, the shorter, stockier one knew the statement was irrefutable. But he also stood the most to lose.

"So this means you take the lead with Richard?" The question was part resignation, part challenge.

"Pom," the older man replied—Pom was a curious name that the short, stocky man intensely disliked, but it had been imposed on him and he lived with it— "You know we have no choice. We have a commitment to keep that we haven't reneged on for the past three generations. Whatever the tensions between us, we all rise or fall together. If we are going to keep our standing here, we need to get beyond our disagreements and act. Besides, you've had Richard pretty much all to yourself these past years."

Pom couldn't argue and didn't try. He was grateful that Cas, the older man with gray hair and gray eyes, didn't make the connection between Pom's influence on Richard and the company's present woes. But he knew they were all thinking it.

Sem, the third member of the party, nodded vigorously in agreement with Cas, and his face was alight with a look of anticipation—the look of someone who has been deprived of something for a long time, and finally sees a window of opportunity to grab it.

"Well, it's time to pay a visit." Cas stood up and the other two stood up with him, one more reluctantly than the other.

Three Visitors to the Corner Office

When Richard looked up from his chair and saw the three figures in front of him, he wasn't sure whether to be startled or amused. He wondered how they had managed to get past Jane; few assistants had been as adept as she at shielding him from unwelcome or unplanned visitors.

In the first moments they stared at each other, before any introductions, he instinctively felt drawn to the one he would come to know as Pom. Of the other two, one struck him as pleasant, and someone he could possibly enjoy getting to know.

The third made him feel decidedly uncomfortable and instinctively uneasy, but at the same time he felt a pang of guilt that maybe he was someone he had ignored and shouldn't have. With his gray hair and gray eyes, Richard had the impression that he saw right through him and beyond him, almost to the point where Richard wanted to turn around and see what he was looking at. He didn't, knowing that there was nothing behind him but the clock tower.

The one he felt an immediate comfort with broke the awkward silence. "I know this is a surprise, and we apologize for coming in unannounced. We know . . ."

With a gesture of impatience, the older one with gray hair and gray eyes—Cas, as Richard would later know him—cut into Pom's introduction.

"You and we know that you don't have much time. We've come to help."

"Much time for what?" Richard's question and posture reflected those of a man who had resigned himself to what he saw as the inevitable. He had even started thinking about engaging the process of selling, something he ruefully acknowledged he would do well.

"To salvage the company. As well as your leadership. And your career, for that matter. Actually, to salvage your leadership so that you can salvage the company."

The bluntness of the comment and the unveiled criticism of his leadership rankled Richard, and he made no attempt to disguise his irritation and impatience with a remark that he hoped would put an end to this incongruous dialog. "I'm not sure if you're aware of this, but the board has just made the decision to sell the company."

"We're well aware of that, and that's why we're here. You can still change the board's decision—or your father's—but you don't have a lot of time."

The mention of his father made Richard suddenly very uncomfort-able, and he wondered how much they knew and how they got their information. This kind of thing could seriously compromise the sale. Nothing had been disclosed beyond the decision to sell, but he didn't want to continue a discussion that might give away more than he wished or intended.

He stood up abruptly, walked to the door and, as he opened it, announced, "Gentlemen, I don't know how you got in here, I don't know who you are, and I don't care to find out. Thank you for the visit and don't bother coming back."

The three stood up, their dignity unimpaired. "We won't. But when you're ready, come and find us in the clock tower. You'll find the door at the bottom unlocked. To anyone else it will be locked. Take the circular staircase to the chambers on the top floor."

On the Way to the Chairman's Office

With characteristic focus, Richard was already making the shift to his role of engineering the sale; he began looking at it as a project and, if this was going to be his last project, he was going to do it well. He wanted to catch his father in the modest office he still maintained in one of the smaller buildings on the corporate campus. Although he seldom ventured on the campus, his father still kept it for the few occasions his role as chairman brought him back again.

When Richard left his office, Jane had already gone home, but he made a mental note to ask her the next day how the three men got past her and into his office.

Cas' last comment about finding them in the clock tower confirmed in Richard's mind that, however sensible they had appeared, he couldn't take them seriously. The clock tower was empty and hadn't been used in years. For all he knew, he had very likely been the last one to go up there, and that was in his mid-teens on one of the many occasions his father brought him to the office when school was out.

He had ventured up there in a spirit of youthful adventurism, and he remembered the old, rather elegant office equipment and the over-stuffed leather chairs in the suite at the top, but it was covered with sheets and pretty much forgotten. He hadn't stayed; he remembered feeling uneasy up there.

As he turned a corner in the main building, he saw Bill, the facilities manager, and it occurred to him to ask him about the stairs to the clock tower.

"Richard, we lost the key to the clock tower some time ago. It's been locked for years. The only time we'd need to get in there would be to do repairs to the clock itself and, for as long as I can remember, it's never needed it—pretty remarkable, now that I come to think of it. Did you want to get in there for some reason?"

"No, though I need you to do something for me—just check to see if it's still locked and let me know one way or the other."

"I'll do it now before I forget and e-mail you." If the request struck Bill as bizarre, it didn't show. Without another comment, Richard pressed on to his father's office.

The Chairman's Office

Richard had always found comfort in the simplicity of his father's office. As he sat waiting for his father, he tried to pinpoint the difference. One difference was obvious: unlike Richard's office, there were no charts or graphs on the walls; he attributed their absence to his father's disengagement from the business but, as he thought about it, he never remembered a lot of graphs on the walls, even when his father was running the business.

This office wasn't as high-tech as his own, but his father was far from technologically illiterate—he couldn't have survived and succeeded in such a high-tech industry without a high measure of technological competence. His technological competence, however, was different from Richard's—Richard was fascinated with the mechanics of the technology itself; his father was more intrigued by its social and economic impact.

As he looked around, he saw more memorabilia; in Richard's office there were none. But the memorabilia were devoid of nostalgia; they carried a message for the future.

Prominently framed was the famous *1984* poster. In 1954, only six years after the publication of Orwell's classic, Richard's grandfather had made everyone read the book and had built up a campaign for a 30-year vision for the company that was anything but Orwellian. There was another poster his father had used based on *2001: A Space Odyssey*; it too projected a 30-year vision. There were others, including one based on the *Back to the Future* movie. His father used movies, he thought to himself, and his grandfather used books. Must be a generational thing.

Between the well-framed posters was a plaque with a biblical quote: "Where there is no vision, the people perish." A likely source of encouragement for his father, it was a definite source of discomfort for Richard.

The room was filled with books. His father was an avid reader. And he would often talk about them. He wondered where his father had found the time to read; Richard certainly didn't have the luxury of time to read.

As he slowly made his way along the bookshelves, he caught sight of the famous "brick." It was a simple brick, but covered in the signatures of his father's leadership team when they had made the gutsy decision to get into microchips. That decision in many ways reshaped the company, and his father had wanted everyone on his team to know that they were rebuilding the company. He often talked about that team as the best one he'd ever worked with; some of its members were on the board.

Other mementos and plaques bore testimony to a lifetime of noble leadership—recognitions for civic contributions, expressions of gratitude, all, however, unostentatiously displayed.

He caught sight of a small cube, about the size of a Rubik's Cube. One side had a diagonal line on it, and the whole cube had the smooth feel of well-worn and well-handled wood. He made a mental note to ask his father what it was. It looked vaguely familiar, but he couldn't pull the image from the recesses of his memory.

"How are you doing?" his father asked, not without concern, as he made his way into the office.

"Trying not to dwell on it." It was a terse statement that conveyed much more than Richard intended. Before his father could comment, he hurriedly went on with the purpose of his visit.

"Now that the board has made the decision, I need to know the time frame. I'm beginning to formulate a plan, but how much time do we have? Also, I wanted to pick your brains about some of the past suitors—could we set some time aside to review what they were looking for and where any of those discussions went? I also want to run by you some of the ones I think we should approach."

The chairman wasn't surprised by his son's focus on the new direction. He had always been one to fight hard and then sign on when the decision was made. He only wished that Richard would pause long enough to learn what he had to learn.

"Nothing is stopping us from moving fairly quickly. In fact, we need to before news of our condition leaks out into the marketplace and our attractiveness is compromised. But realistically, the provisions to remove the poison pill will take six months from the next board meeting, so we have essentially nine months."

Richard had forgotten about the poison pill. His grandfather had been so concerned about a premature and hasty sale of the business before it could reach the next generation that he had included a series of elaborate and complicated provisions that up to now had been adequate to dissipate the interest of otherwise aggressive and hungry suitors. Most of all, they were designed to discourage the family from selling and, until now, they had succeeded.

For the first time, there was a flicker of hope within Richard. Getting a clear sense of the time frame put a different picture on it. When the three visitors had said he didn't have much time, he took it as not enough time; nine months wasn't long, but it might be enough to change people's—the board's, his father's—mind. He hadn't given his three visitors a thought since he'd been in his father's office and their memory was a surprising intrusion.

Questions in the
Clock Tower

D o you think he'll come?" Sem was worried the opening he
had seen would begin to close.

Cas looked up from the entry he was making in his journal.

"Absolutely. He has to."

"Do you think he'll respond?"

"I believe so. This has certainly caught his attention."

"What if he doesn't respond?"

"He, like the rest of his family, will be very wealthy, and he'll spend
the rest of his life trying to assuage his sense of failure."

The Clock Tower Door

Richard returned to his office to pick up his briefcase and check his e-mail. All could wait, he told himself, but he was curious about the e-mail from the facilities manager, a brief message with no surprises:

> "The door is good and locked, and we'd need to get a key made for it. The lock is pretty much rusted in, and it will take more than just getting a key made. It would be a shame to damage the door—that's a pretty solid piece of wood. They don't make them like that anymore. Let me know if you want me to do something about it."

Without responding, Richard logged off and left.

As he opened the back door to his car and threw in his briefcase, he looked up at the clock tower. He hesitated briefly, then closed the door and walked slowly across the courtyard to the entrance of the clock tower. This part of the corporate campus had the feel of a New England prep school, and he felt very much like a furtive schoolboy about to trespass on forbidden territory.

The main entrance to the clock tower was a heavy oak door that was permanently unlocked. He pushed it open and entered the small foyer that contained two more doors. He ignored the one on the right (a modern-looking door that led to a room used as a supplies closet) and focused on the imposing oak door on the left.

Richard admired the heavy wrought-iron hinges that prominently and firmly held the door to the frame. He inspected the lock, which, contrary to Bill's assessment, didn't show any signs of rust. In the middle of the door was an old wrought-iron ring that raised the latch on the inside, once the door was unlocked.

Richard somewhat mechanically turned the ring, and gave a push. To his surprise, it offered no resistance. The door swung gently open without a sound.

The Clock Tower
Staircase

Before him was a small, compact foyer, with uneven hand-crafted stone slabs as flooring. An arched opening framed the entrance to the circular staircase, and Richard stared at the worn stone steps and the rope handrail that disappeared into the darkness of the stairwell.

If he were to turn back, this would be the time. But the magnetic pull of the clock tower was now stronger than ever, and the curiosity in his head was winning over the fear in his heart. Before venturing up the staircase, however, Richard checked his escape route. He closed the door gently, looking for a key on the inside (there wasn't one) and opening it again to make sure he wouldn't get trapped inside.

Satisfied, he faced the staircase and, with a deep breath, started up the stairs, slowly, carefully, as much out of fear as out of caution.

The circular staircase seemed endless, and his grip on the rope was tight. At each floor, a heavy wooden door in a short recess off to the side of the stairwell was secured not only with a heavy lock but with additional planks nailed across the frame, discouraging anyone from even the thought of penetrating the forbidding barrier. As he passed the lower floors, he thought he could figure out roughly where these uninviting doors led to in the adjoining building, but as he climbed higher, he became less and less sure. He had no more inclination to penetrate the mysteries of these doors than when he had made the same venture as a teenager. As the stairs continued, the constant circular pattern of the stairwell became confusing, and he lost a sense of how far and how long he had climbed.

When he finally circled the last bend, he was startled by a shaft of light escaping from under the dark door that stood as a stern sentinel at the top of the seemingly endless stairs. It wasn't natural light; it was dusk outside. The light had caught him at eye level, and he climbed the last few steps to reach the short space that leveled out in front of the door. He stood motionless, his hand on the door knob, hesitating. He'd come this far, and turning back was unthinkable. With a decisive gesture, Richard turned the knob and stepped into the brightly lit room.

A Visitor to
the Clock Tower

The light came from several old but elegant lamps strategically placed around the room. The furniture was pretty much as Richard remembered it, though without the sheets covering them. The walls between the windows were lined with richly stained wooden bookcases, filled with books. He thought for a moment he had stepped into the faculty room of an Oxford college.

Cas and Sem were sitting comfortably in large stuffed chairs, reading. They looked up from their books and watched Richard as his eyes swept around the room and absorbed the surroundings.

"Glad you came, Richard," Cas said as he stood up to greet him. Sem rose with him, gesturing to one of the empty old leather armchairs. Richard ignored the offer; he was too keyed up to sit down and the questions churned so quickly in his mind that he didn't know where to begin.

"Who are you?" he finally blurted out.

"We'll have plenty of time for introductions. For now, you need to know that we are firmly committed to your success. Partly altruistically, partly out of self-preservation and partly to honor the commitments we have made to the generations that preceded you. We have been involved with every generation of this company since its inception, and we don't want to see our investment evaporate."

After a pause, he added almost as an afterthought, "My name is Cas. This is Sem." Sem nodded and smiled warmly.

"Where's the other one?" Richard asked, especially since he had the recollection of feeling the most comfortable around him.

"Pom? He'll be with us soon. We might as well get started. We can start without him." Cas was actually glad Pom wasn't in the room; this might make a difficult transition easier for him.

"Let's start by your telling us what's going on. The board just met this afternoon and made the decision to sell. What led up to that decision?"

Cas and Sem waited for Richard to collect his thoughts. Cautiously at first, but with increasing abandon, he spent the next 20 minutes, almost uninterrupted, unloading the events of the past three years and his responses to them. Prompted occasionally by a question from Cas or Sem (more to help Richard express himself than to clarify his statements), he was surprised by the candor of his self-expression and, at the end, he felt cleansed. This, he thought, is what a confessional must feel like.

Nothing Richard had said was new to Cas or Sem, or would have been to Pom if he'd been there.

Just as Cas was about to respond, a small door that Richard hadn't noticed before lurched open brusquely and a gruff-looking Pom emerged carrying a hefty wrench and wearing a pair of well-soiled overalls. When he caught sight of Richard, he felt compelled to give an explanation.

"Been doing some maintenance work on the clock. Need to do it to keep people from coming up here. Not that they would see anything, but the less they think about coming up here, the better."

Richard thought back to when he had come up here as a teenager. "Were you . . ." he started, but then thought better of it.

"Yes, Richard, we were here then," Sem answered the incomplete question. "We figured you'd be back some time."

For Pom's benefit, Cas summarized the conversation thus far, and then proceeded with his own comments.

"Richard, thank you for the honesty of your remarks, and rest assured that we will speak with equal candor. You are here because your leadership is in trouble and, because your leadership is in trouble, your company is in trouble."

Richard wasn't quite ready to make the direct connection between the company's present condition and his own leadership.

"What about market conditions and economic downturns?" He started with a measure of defensiveness; with each question, the defensiveness increasingly gave way to aggressiveness. "What about technological innovation that puts our business at risk? What about the fickleness of the capital markets? What about the risk inherent in R&D decisions, especially in an industry such as ours? What about the financial pressures they create? What about poor employee performance? What about the competition's predatory recruiting practices? What about competing personal agendas? What about..?"

Before the litany could get any longer, Cas interrupted him. "Every one of those is a leadership issue. You can't change market conditions or avoid economic downturns, you can't prevent the competition from innovating, but the company's response is a leadership issue."

Cas paused to give weight to the next comment. "One of the premises by which we operate is that what goes on inside the heads of an organization's leaders is the most significant thing about that organization. What's going on inside your head is the key to what's going on now."

When everything was going well, that was a premise Richard could live with; it was harder when it wasn't.

Taking advantage of the pause, Cas pushed in the direction he wanted to go in. "Richard, let's talk about your leadership. How would you describe your strengths as a leader?"

"Direct, take charge, deliver results, good organizer, strong project management skills, good grasp of the financials, good problem solver, no nonsense, tough but fair . . ." Richard ran out of qualifiers.

"We wouldn't argue with any of those," Cas concurred, "and I doubt if any of your people would either."

After a pause, he asked, "What would your people say about your deficiencies as a leader?"

Richard looked blank. He had never thought about the question.

"What do you think they need that you're not providing?"

Richard still looked blank.

Cas tried a different tack to help Richard respond to what was obviously a tough question. "What qualities did you see in your father as a leader?"

Richard thought about his father's office and the vision posters. "He was forward-looking, I'd say. A visionary."

"Would your people say that about you?"

"No." He recognized that he was much more operationally focused than his father.

"What else do you see in your father?"

Richard thought for a moment, and then ventured, "Well, I'm not sure how to put this, but he was very consistent. You knew what he expected from you. In a way, he was predictable."

"Would your people say that about you?" Cas was relentless.

"Yes, I'd say I'm pretty consistent."

"I'd agree with you; you are. The difference between you and your father is not so much in the consistency of your values, but in the articulation of those values. Your father spoke frequently about what was important to him. You don't. And when you don't articulate them, you don't clarify them."

The directness of Cas' comment silenced Richard and Cas waited to gauge his response as Richard sat down heavily in one of the few straight-backed chairs. Richard didn't like it, but he was assimilating it.

"What else would you say about your father?"

Richard thought about the brick in his father's office, with all those signatures. "He had a way of getting people on the same page. And he was gutsy. He made some courageous decisions. He wasn't scared of taking big risks, but they were also well-weighed."

"Would they say that about you?" The uncomfortable question again. Richard squirmed in his seat.

"No." He realized much of what drove him was preserving what he'd been given, and he was beginning to see that in trying to preserve it, he was losing it.

It was Pom's turn to speak up. He was proud of Richard and his own indirect, invisible influence over Richard, but he also knew that Richard and the company were headed for a serious derailment if he didn't change.

"Richard, let me let you in on a secret. Cas and I have been at logger-heads over you these past few years. In fact, we fight most of the time anyway, and the tension we create makes life difficult for Sem. Cas and I—in fact all three of us—just focus on different dimensions of leadership and, most of the time, none of us is willing to let go."

Richard didn't catch Pom's furtive sideways look at Cas; Pom knew that, in reality, he was the one having the most difficulty letting go. For his part, Richard had been following Pom's comments with ut-most sympathy; he'd have a hard time getting on with Cas if he had been in Pom's shoes. As that thought crossed his mind, he felt a pang of guilt and looked at Cas apologetically. Cas remained inscrutable.

"But this is too serious for us to continue the fight," Pom continued, "and I have come to terms with the fact that you need much more than I have given you. Or rather, what you need is not what I can give you."

Richard's puzzled expression at Pom's comment elicited further explanation, but it came in the form of a question.

"Richard, when have you felt at your most comfortable in a leadership role?"

That was easy. "When I manage a project. When I led the IT department, or Sales and R&D for that matter."

"And of the qualities you mentioned earlier about your own leadership style, which of those did you need for those leadership roles?"

To refresh his memory, he added, "You mentioned things such as being direct, taking charge, delivering results, being a good organizer, having strong project management skills, having a good grasp of the financials, being a good problem solver, being a no-nonsense, tough but fair kind of leader."

"I would say pretty much all of them."

"I'd agree—those strike me as pretty impressive qualities too—and pretty appropriate for those kinds of leadership roles."

Much as he liked Pom and the compliments he was getting, he wasn't sure he liked the direction Pom was going in. Pom's next statement confirmed it.

"Richard, tell us again, what were the qualities you recognized in your father?"

Reluctantly, Richard thought back to his father's office and the responses it elicited earlier in the conversation. "Vision. Gutsy decision making. Pulling a good team around him. Being clear on his values."

"And as I recollect your responses, you didn't rate yourself very high on these attributes."

By this point, Richard was beginning to feel betrayed by Pom. He thought their kinship would have spared him this painful self-exposure.

As if reading Richard's mind, Pom sensed it was time to bring some clarity to the line of questioning he and Cas had been pursuing. "Richard, the reason you and I connect is because we are drawn to the same kind of leadership, and the reason you and I have a hard time with Cas is that his leadership focus challenges ours. You and I are operationally driven; in fact, my whole leadership focus is operational leadership. What you need is a good dose of Cas' organizational leadership focus. The difficulties you are now facing are in large measure because you haven't made the transition. It's time for me to let you go, Richard. And it's also time for you to let go."

There. He had said it. Pom looked over at Cas, who smiled and nodded appreciatively.

There was silence while Richard absorbed Pom's statement and while Pom leaned back to breathe more evenly.

After what he considered an adequately therapeutic silence, Cas stood up and moved over to a flip chart Richard hadn't noticed before.

"Richard, there are in fact three dimensions of leadership. Pom mentioned two—organizational leadership and operational leadership. There is a third dimension."

Cas had already written "organizational leadership" and "operational leadership" on the flip chart sheet and was about to write the third when Richard interrupted him.

"When people talk about the difference between managers and leaders, is this what they mean?"

"Yes." It was Pom who responded, not without a trace of irritation in his voice. "And the distinction is confusing, because people who make that distinction elevate what they call 'leadership' at the expense of what they call 'management.' They oversimplify the tension by saying 'managers do things right, leaders do the right thing'—a statement you have most likely heard, since enough people make it. The problem is that it doesn't validate or recognize what managers do. And that's why we prefer to talk about organizational leadership and operational leadership; both are legitimate and valid forms of leadership if applied in the right context."

"Without detracting from Pom's comments," Cas resumed, "it's important to note that operational leadership is the easiest to default to because it's the first kind of leadership we learn in the workplace. As a frontline manager or first-time supervisor, we are very operationally focused. Unfortunately, we don't always adjust as our responsibilities increase."

Always the one to bring it back to Richard's circumstances, Cas added, "And that, by the way, is the trap you have fallen into."

Not wanting to dwell there any longer, Richard asked, "What about the third one?"

"The third is people leadership. That's Sem's focus."

Cas tossed the marker over to Sem, who took his place at the flip chart. He had the energy of one who held the mike after years of deprivation.

"Richard, you and I haven't had much of a chance to get acquainted, but I certainly hope we do. You need what I bring as much as you need what Cas offers."

This latest exposure of Richard's needs was said with enough grace and gentleness that Richard could assimilate it more readily. Besides it was all beginning to make sense.

"Let me summarize it for all of us," Sem continued. Turning the flip chart to a clean page, he drew three circles that intersected in the middle. To each circle, he gave a name: the top one he called "organizational leadership," the lower left one he called "operational leadership" and the bottom right one he called "people leadership."

And then in large letters, he wrote in the middle of the diagram where the three circles overlapped, "A Well-Led Organization."

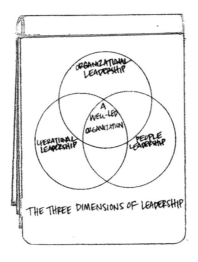

"Richard, what do you think would happen if one of those circles were missing? What about organizational leadership?"

Sem drew the three circles again, but this time without any overlap from organizational leadership.

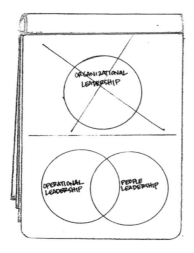

"Not much direction, not much sense of purpose, not much clarity . . . a lot like us," Richard added ruefully.

"A well-run Titanic with no one on the bridge watching for icebergs," Cas offered.

Richard didn't like the analogy with the Titanic, but it was apt.

"What happens if you take out the operational leadership circle?" Sem redrew the three circles, this time with operational leadership detached.

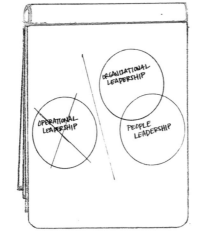

"A great sense of vision, but lots of duplication, inefficiencies, wastage, incompetencies—in fact a lot of frustration." That, Richard thought thankfully as he rattled off the list of negative side effects, was not something he wrestled with.

Unfortunately, Richard realized, no one seemed to want to dwell on these attributes, and Sem pressed on with the next question.

"What happens if you take out the people leadership circle?" This time, he drew the people leadership circle detached from the others.

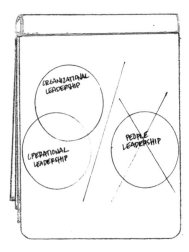

Richard's expression betrayed the uncertainty of his response and, spurred on by the candor in the room, he found himself saying, "I'm not sure I understand what you mean by people leadership."

"It's not just being nice to people, Richard, and having good people skills, which is what most people boil it down to. In fact, some leaders who do this well don't have particularly good people skills, at least not naturally."

Richard was relieved that his admission of ignorance wasn't dismissed as stupidity.

"It's much more a question of knowing how to bring out the best in the people you lead," Sem went on, "and to do that, you need to know what they are good at and put them in the roles where they can do what they are good at. You need to be clear in your expectations, you need to provide the kind of environment that will keep them energized and motivated, and you need to be focused on developing them. That's what we mean by people leadership. It's more important to be intentional than to be nice," and as an afterthought, he said, "but it helps if you can be nice, too."

As Sem rattled off these bullet points, Richard couldn't think of one he did consciously or deliberately. When you hired someone, you assumed they were good enough to do the job. When they were in it, you assumed they knew what to do. Motivation is an issue of internal drive, he reasoned to himself, and development was each person's own responsibility.

Sem interrupted Richard's train of thought by repeating his question. "So what happens when you take out people leadership?"

Richard had been trying hard to dismiss this dimension of leadership, but the question forced him to confront the reality of his own experience.

"More turnover," he ventured as he thought about the company in the past few years.

"Why would people leave?" Sem asked.

"They don't like the job. They're in the wrong job and don't fit . . ."

"They've been put in the wrong job," Sem corrected him, "but we'll clarify that later. What else?"

Richard thought back to Sem's oral bullet points. "They don't feel they're being developed, perhaps . . ."

"Absolutely. If people feel you care about their development, they'll think you care about them. And they'll stay. Remember, people quit bosses, not companies."

That last statement startled Richard. He couldn't help thinking about the two members of his leadership team who had quit. They'd been with the company well before he took over. He had never questioned his responsibility in their departure and the thought that they had quit him, not the company, was uncomfortable, to say the least.

"That's good for a start," Sem said, sensing that Richard needed time to digest what was turning out to be a radical assessment of his leadership. "We'll be coming back to that anyway."

Cas stood up and looked at the circles on the flip chart. "Richard, which one of those scenarios fits you?"

There was that uncomfortable question again. As if he wasn't feeling uncomfortable enough without having to voice it.

"Weak organizational leadership and weak people leadership," Richard said meekly, barely audible.

"And that's why we're here. Or more accurately, that's why *you're* here."

Whether it was a genuine question or a final surge of defensiveness, Richard wondered out loud whether his leadership was really perceived as that deficient. "I wish I knew what they really thought about my leadership."

"Ask them," Cas said.

"Ask them?"

"Yes. Great leaders have huge amounts of self-awareness and they get that self-awareness by soliciting feedback. They view feedback as a gift, whatever shape it comes in. So ask them."

The idea intrigued Richard. "How would I do that? I don't want anything as complex or time-consuming as a 360-degree feedback, but I do want something meaningful."

"Try this," Sem suggested. "Ask your leadership team collectively to make a list of what they want you to start doing, what they want you to stop doing and what they want you to keep doing. Have them write it on flip charts and leave the room while they do it. When they're done, come back and respond. Be open for anything and be gracious."

A scary prospect, Richard thought, but he wanted the feedback. "Be open for anything," however, wasn't very reassuring.

The Library

I t had been a long time since he'd been in a library. As a student, the library was the place of last resort, not the place of first choice. Librarians had always struck him as gray and faceless, far removed from real life and action. But as his project progressed, so too did his appreciation for the skill and expertise they exercised as they guided him from one database to another, from one reference book to another, from one journal to another, and from one author to another.

As the morning wore on and Richard's odyssey lengthened, it seemed the grayness of the building and its guardians was gradually replaced by an energy and color he hadn't seen before, much as the tones in Van Gogh's paintings as he migrated from the somber colors of northern Europe to the vivid colors of southern France. He was beginning to see a lot of things he hadn't seen before, he thought to himself, so this shouldn't come as any surprise.

The perception of his current surroundings wasn't the only metamorphosis taking place. He had come into the library clutching a list of potential buyers and a well-defined list of considerations. He was looking for a buyer that would see the company as a highly strategic acquisition; the holy grail of his odyssey was to uncover the one who needed his company the most. On his list were some obvious names—the heavy hitters such as Moon MicroSystems, Aptel, Synchtronics, Nell Computers, and Moteurolah (the French conglomerate)—as well as a host of smaller but significant players. With characteristic organization, he had developed a matrix with the names of the companies across the top and the list of considerations down the side—considerations such as their investment in R&D, the number of patents they owned, the extent of their off-shore manufacturing, their supply-chain-management practices, and so on.

But the metamorphosis was taking him out of the confines of his matrix. The more he uncovered about the competition and the industry players, the less he thought about them as companies and the more he thought about the industry itself. In the process, he uncovered some players he had never heard of—small but innovative companies such as IQ^2, a company with some impressive patents and what seemed like an aggressive research agenda. It was undercapitalized and not a candidate as an acquirer, but it was intriguing nonetheless.

Like a camera pulling back from the close-up of a wild flower to the broad sweep of a panoramic vista, he began looking at the industry's landscape through a different set of lenses, until finally he pushed aside his matrix and pulled out his notepad. The questions began pouring out on the paper. What did competitive advantage mean in this industry? What was it now? What would it become? What were the Achilles' heels of the big players? What new technology would reconfigure the industry? Where would the unexpected new entrants come from? Who were on the fringes of the industry and heading inside? What demographics were shaping the industry? What would the industry look like in 30 years' time? What could this company look like in 30 years' time?

The last two questions had him sitting bolt upright. These, he realized, were the kinds of questions his father would raise. And, with a pang of guilt, he also realized that he should have been asking them three years ago.

Such was the depth of his absorption that it had silenced the usual clamors of caffeine deficiency and the inevitable demands of an empty stomach, but before those clamors could be heard, the metamorphosis was complete. His quest was now a different one, and he knew what he had to do.

The Executive Team

As Richard sat down at the end of the table, he realized how uncharacteristically unprepared he was. He didn't have the list of focused and pointed questions he typically fired at his team; the events of the past few days had been so consuming and unsettling that he now questioned almost every response and initiative that previously had been second nature to him.

"Er . . . I have a question for you." Actually, he had many and he wasn't sure where to start.

His team sensed Richard's hesitation and it caught them by surprise. This wasn't the normal start to one of these meetings, which if they could speak their minds, were more interrogation than meeting.

"I'd like to set aside our usual agenda and probe into some other questions that have been on my mind." In the pause that followed, the unease grew stronger still as they wondered which direction this interrogation was going.

"I'm trying to get a better handle on how we are doing in the industry. How are we doing? How are we doing as a company? What's good about us? What's bad? What are we particularly good at? What does the competition think of us? Heck, what do our customers think of us?"

As the questions piled up on top of each other, the unease was replaced with confusion; these were not the kind of questions Richard typically asked. The hesitation around the table was not from a lack of ideas but from an uncertainty about the safety of sharing them.

Partly to fill the void and partly to complete his train of thought, he continued, "I've been trying to go further than that—not only how are we doing, but how could we do? How could we reshape this industry? What would that take? What do we need to be looking for and what do we need to do or be to become the type of company that could reshape the industry?"

As the questions rolled off his tongue, the hesitation continued. This wasn't a Richard they knew. Looking at their uncertain expressions, Richard recognized that he hadn't given them any context for these questions, so he continued by describing the hours he had spent in the library, though he was careful not to let on that the research had been initiated by the quest for a buyer. He even asked them about IQ^2 and his finance director mentioned he had a friend who had worked there.

The conversation slowly began to open up, but for the most part it was the sequential expression of a few widely accepted platitudes. It was a cautious discussion, not what he had expected. It gathered some momentum, but it never reached the intensity of lively debate he was hoping for.

They had the same level of spontaneity, he mused, as a group of kids told to play under the muzzle of a gun—going through the motions, but without much enthusiasm.

Richard's growing disappointment, however, was not directed at them; it was directed at himself. On the one hand, he realized that their reluctance to debate was a reflection of his past unwillingness to tolerate it and, on the other, he recognized how little he knew about them and how much talent he had overlooked.

The discussion bumped along laboriously, fitfully. It needed a change of direction; more importantly, he needed to show them he could be trusted with their candor.

"Look," he interrupted, "I appreciate your ideas, but I'm not sure we're getting very far. And that's not your fault," he added, as he looked at their probing expressions.

"Besides, I had something else I wanted to ask you about. We've been talking about the company and the industry, but I'm just as interested in what you think about my leadership. I recently talked with three men who asked me some tough questions, and their questions made me wonder what you thought of my leadership. I would really like to know. I also know that I haven't in the past made it easy for you to express those kinds of thoughts. I want to change that."

He paused, trying to gauge their response. Their expressions hadn't changed, so he pressed on.

"I know that you'd have a hard time telling me directly and I'm beginning to understand why. So I'm going to ask you to do something different. If you would, come up with responses to these three questions: What do you want me to stop doing? What do you want me to keep doing? And what do you want me to start doing? If you would write them up on a flip chart, I'll come back when you're finished and respond to them."

"And I promise I won't go on a witch hunt," he added. "I'm serious about wanting your honesty."

They looked at each other with a mixture of hesitation and anticipation; with some, he thought, it might have been gleefulness.

Richard walked over to the door. "By the way," he said with his hand on the doorknob, "make sure you have one person doing the scribing so that I can't recognize anyone's handwriting."

The Wailing Wall

As Richard paced up and down in front of his window, he realized what it must be like for a defendant waiting for a jury's decision. This was taking much longer than he thought; what was taking them so long?

When they finally buzzed him in his office, he made his way slowly to the conference room. He wasn't ready for the spectacle of a repapered wall.

Kathy, Richard's vice president for procurement and supply chain management, had been designated as the scribe and became the group's spokesperson.

"Richard," she said, pointing to three sheets in the middle of the wall, "these are the main ideas we came up with in response to your questions. These other sheets," she waved to a series of other sheets covered with less legible scribbling, "were our first pass before we distilled them into these main points. We kept the others in case you wanted to look at them, but the essence is on these three sheets."

She paused a moment, while Richard scanned the less legible scribbling of the other sheets, then focused on the three sheets in the middle.

Kathy paused to give Richard a moment to absorb the data on the sheets and to try to gauge his response. To her, his face was inscrutable; to him, it was stoic. "Richard," she pressed on courageously, "the way we did this is that we each took some time on our own to write down our thoughts, and we brainstormed while I wrote on these original flip charts. After *that*, we tried to capture all these ideas more succinctly, and that's what these three sheets represent.

"Richard, we stayed with your three questions, but as we shared our responses, we realized they broke down into different categories. That's what we put on this flip chart." Kathy pointed to another sheet to the side.

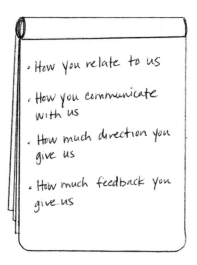

· How you relate to us

· How you communicate with us

· How much direction you give us

· How much feedback you give us

Richard stood there, trying to sort out his emotions and his responses. This was worse than he thought, and his initial response was anything but charitable. But he remembered Sem's advice: be gracious. And no witch-hunts, he had promised.

"I can't say this is easy or comfortable," Richard finally said, "but I think this is going to be helpful. Thank you for the candor of your feedback."

What Richard wanted most of all at that point was to have them leave and give him time to lick his wounds. But remembering Sem's strong endorsement of the need for feedback, he sat down and continued.

"It would help me if you could give me some examples."

Slowly, cautiously, mostly through the anonymity of Kathy as a mouthpiece, one example followed another. In some cases the context revealed the source. Some comments made sense; others didn't. The ones that didn't, however, didn't seem worth fighting over. He was conscious of how defensive every clarification sounded.

After half an hour, Kathy graciously suggested that he needed more time on his own to ponder the feedback he'd received. She was relieved that he hadn't fought back, but she didn't want to push their luck.

They left quickly and, in the silence of the empty room, Richard stared at the writing on the wall.

Confession may be good for the soul, but it wasn't doing much for his spirits.

"This," he thought as he sat there looking at the flip chart sheets redecorating the conference room, "is my wailing wall."

The Meaning of the Writing on the Wall

A despondent Richard sat slumped in one of the over stuffed leather chairs and looked down glumly at the faded rug in the middle of the room. "Some gift," he muttered, barely audible. Faint though it was, it was still audible to the other three, all in pensive postures in the over-stuffed chairs. All three knew what he was referring to.

"So you've seen the writing on the wall, eh?" Pom ventured with a wry smile.

"What bothers you about the feedback?" Sem asked.

"Everything. They have a pretty low opinion of my leadership."

"What was good about it?"

"Nothing."

"Yes, there was. What did they want you to keep doing?"

"Some nebulous stuff that they probably put there to keep me from going off the deep end."

"What was it?"

"It was about being direct, being honest, keeping my standards, that kind of stuff."

"That sounds pretty significant to me."

Sem's comment didn't sound very convincing to Richard, but it raised a quizzical eyebrow.

"Richard, when someone tells you that they want you to keep being honest and to maintain your standards, what are they saying about you?"

"Well, if they're being sincere, that I'm dependable, I suppose."

"That's pretty significant. They recognize you as someone fundamentally trustworthy. If those hadn't been there, I'm not sure we'd hold much hope for you and I'm not sure we'd want to work with you."

The thought was a sobering one. Richard knew that Sem meant it.

"The good news," Sem went on, "is that what is harder to change doesn't need to be changed—the character stuff such as honesty and so on. So let's look at what they do want you to change—let's start with what they want you to start doing. Do you see any themes in what they listed?"

Richard pulled out his notes and consulted the list. "There's the 'big picture' stuff, as they put it—giving a sense of direction, being focused on the big picture, talking about the big picture—I suppose that means not just having a sense of direction but also talking about it—leading the company, not the operations." Richard paused and looked up from his list.

"Even the one about 'valuing non-operations functions' would fit into that category," Sem added. "Are those things you just identified something you can learn?"

"Well, I'd hope so."

"Exactly. If you knew what to do, you could do it."

Richard nodded, and Sem continued. "What other themes do you see?"

"Micro-managing seems to be another one. They seem to think I treat them as if they were two levels below their current roles."

"Do you?" Sem asked.

"Not consciously, but they must think I do."

"Is it related to the previous theme you identified—about the big picture?"

Richard thought about that for a moment, and the connection suddenly seemed obvious. If he were focused on the big picture, it would be much harder to micro-manage them. He played out the thought with Sem, and then concluded, "Perhaps they feel I'm treating them as two levels below their role because I'm operating two levels below mine—maybe more."

Sem and the others paused to add weight to the perceptiveness of his insight.

"Profound observation, Richard," Cas finally said. "If you learn the skills associated with clarifying the direction, you'll inevitably be less inclined to micromanage your leadership team. And as Sem pointed out, it is a learned behavior. They are not asking you to change your personality."

Richard took the positive reinforcement with gratitude, especially coming from Cas, but the list still bothered him. "Thank you . . . but there's still stuff on this list that isn't as easy to change as you make it sound."

"Such as? What other themes do you see in this list?"

"They want me to develop them. I don't have a clue how to start."

"But if you knew what to do, wouldn't you be able to do it? In other words, it's not knowing what to do that's the hang up . . . isn't it?"

"Well, what would I have to do?"

"You'd have to be deliberate about it. You'd need to sit down with them, find out what their aspirations are, and together figure out a way to get there. You'd need to help them identify some goals and establish some type of plan with some measure of accountability to reach those goals. And you'd need to tailor it to each one individually. There's more to it than that, but it's not that complicated."

When Sem presented it like that, it didn't seem insurmountable. "Well, I suppose I could learn that."

Then Richard thought about the list again. "But what about listening? I'm a terrible listener and they told me so. I already knew that. How can I develop them if I don't know how to listen?"

"Well, let's look at that one," Sem said. "What did they say about listening?"

"Actually, quite a lot—they want me to start listening, which clearly suggests in their minds that I've never done it."

"That's true, and they're probably right. There are several other things on that list that suggest you don't listen—devaluing different opinions, stifling discussion, being always right, and so on." Cas' characteristic bluntness was nothing new now to Richard, but he was also getting used to the affirmation that followed. "But the question is this: if you were focusing on the big picture and leading the company, and if you were focusing on their development, wouldn't that make it easier for you to listen?"

"Yes, it probably would—I would have to."

"Exactly—half the battle in listening is realizing how important it is. You'll then find it a whole lot easier to learn some skills that will make you a better listener. It is true that some people are naturally gifted listeners—they stay focused, they ask good questions, and they communicate that they value the person they are listening to. But that doesn't mean that the rest of us can't improve our own listening skills. So again, to Sem's point, it's a learned skill."

"Facilitated by the right motivation," Sem interjected.

"Richard," Cas continued, "you identified several key areas their comments fall into—thinking big picture, developing them, listening to them. We didn't address the trust factor—they asked you to start trusting them—but if you learn the skills we have been talking about, you'll find it much easier to trust them—and they will feel trusted."

"Richard, let's hit the pause button a moment." It was Sem's turn. "Tell us how you are absorbing all of this. Is this making sense and do you feel that you can learn some of these skills?"

Richard thought for a moment, then in measured tones expressed a mixture of hope about the possibility of changing but some uncertainty about his ability to sustain it. Sem responded with a reaffirmation of the principle they were drawing out.

"All these are skills. And skills can be learned and developed. We may not have the talent of a Tiger Woods, but it doesn't stop us from becoming pretty effective golfers by getting the right knowledge and developing the right skills by practicing them. You may not be a natural listener, but you can certainly learn to become a better one. You haven't given direction because up to now you didn't know how; but with the right knowledge, it wouldn't be difficult for you to give them the kind of direction they're asking from you."

"Richard," Cas said, "don't hear us as saying that character isn't important. It is. Very important. In fact, it's critical. But that's not what they're addressing in their comments. They've identified a set of skills you're missing."

Richard looked over the list again. Rough though it looked, it wasn't without hope and, as he licked his wounds, he was beginning to think that they might not be as deep as he thought. The vital signs were still intact.

"Richard, again, they're not asking you to change your personality. They're asking you to learn and use skills you currently aren't."

At that point, it dawned on Richard that they had referred to his wailing wall without, to his knowledge, ever seeing it. A little unnerving, but at the same time reassuring.

"It's time to get more practical," Sem finally pronounced.

The Cube

"Richard, let's recap what you've learned. Give us a summary of what you've discovered since the first time we met."

Richard thought back to that first meeting in his office, then the first time he had pushed open the door to the clock tower and climbed the well-worn stone stairs up to their chambers. It seemed a long time ago, but it was only a matter of months, barely. His thoughts became a logical and chronological account of what he'd been learning and experiencing since that gloomy and somber board meeting.

"That's a good synopsis," Sem said when he'd finished. "You've made some important steps. Most importantly, you have identified the three types of leadership every organization needs in order to be led effectively. In summary, organizational leadership is about organizational effectiveness and relevance . . ." He slowed down as he read aloud what he was writing on the flip chart. "Operational leadership is about organizational efficiency and responsiveness . . . People leadership is about individual effectiveness and productivity."

He finished with a flourish and, standing back, he continued. "Now it's time to see how they connect and relate to each other—the key to exercising great leadership. You also know that each of the three of us—Cas, Pom and I—focus on a different element."

Sem looked down at the rug and paused while he collected his thoughts. "Richard, you may have wondered how we got our names." Everything about his encounter with his three mentors had been bizarre, so he was ready for some revelation of ancient intergalactic ancestry.

"It's very simple. They're acronyms."

"Acronyms?" This wasn't an explanation Richard was expecting.

"Yes, acronyms. In fact from now on, think of our names as capitalized."

"Capitalized?" Richard interrupted.

"Yes, Richard, capitalized." SEM was beginning to wonder whether they were coaching a parrot.

"That's not out of ego," he continued, "but to help you remember what you need to be doing as a leader."

Without dwelling on the rationale for capitalization, SEM launched into his explanation. "Let's start with CAS and POM. You've already picked up the tension between them, and you'll see even more clearly why they have such a tense relationship. Now here's what CAS stands for . . ." Back he went to the flip chart, reading as he wrote:

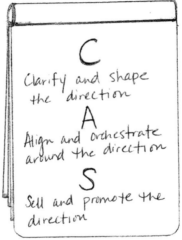

C
Clarify and shape the direction

A
Align and orchestrate around the direction

S
Sell and promote the direction

"Now, where is CAS' focus—inside the organization or outside?"

Richard remembered their first meeting and the sense he had of CAS looking through him into the far distance. He thought of his father whose focus was constantly outside, and far ahead.

"Outside." It was a no-brainer.

"That's right. And which is POM's?"

"Inside."

"That's right. And here's what POM's initials stand for . . ." SEM went back to the flip chart and, as he wrote (and read aloud), POM obligingly pinned CAS' sheet to the nearest wall.

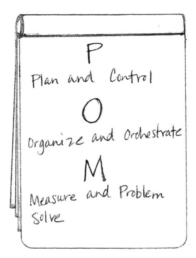

"CAS' focus is external, POM's is internal. CAS' concern is organizational effectiveness, POM's is organizational efficiency. CAS thinks about the 'why' of the organization, POM thinks about the 'how.' CAS is concerned with the organization's external relevance, POM is concerned with the organization's internal viability."

"You can see why we fight," POM interjected, with a faint smile at the corner of his mouth.

"Let's take a look at CAS' role in more detail. What do you think it means to 'clarify and shape direction'?"

Richard thought about his father's office, his own time spent in the library, and the whole notion of thinking about the company's contribution and relevance.

"Developing a sense of vision, having something to aspire to as a company, clarifying why we exist as a company, giving the company a sense of . . . well, direction."

"Yes. That's good. Can you think of anything else?"

"Isn't that enough? What else is there?"

"Well, it's not just knowing where you want to go, but it's also knowing what type of company you want to be as you pursue that direction. In other words, it's also about the company's values. That's why we talk about *shaping* the direction. So . . . what do you think the company has valued in the past?"

Richard thought for a moment, but it didn't take him long to come up with one that was glaringly obvious.

"Innovation. This company has always valued innovation."

"Yes, it has, very much so. Does anything else come to mind?" Several things came to mind, but Richard didn't want to voice any he wasn't sure were genuine and deeply held. The next prompt came from CAS.

"Richard, what value do you think drove the board's decision to sell the company?"

The answer came to mind immediately; it was a little harder voicing it.

"The absence of good leadership," he said quietly.

"That must be a strong value if they made such a drastic decision."

For Richard's sake, they didn't dwell on it, and SEM moved on. "What about aligning? What does that suggest to you?"

"Aligning all the pieces of the organization around the purpose, values and vision—around the direction."

"Exactly. Not just the pieces, but also the people. You want everyone committed to the same purpose, vision and values, as well as making sure that all the 'pieces,' as you put it—such as recruitment, development, systems, structures, and so on—all facilitate and are aligned with the pursuit of the purpose, values and vision."

As Richard listened to SEM, the enormity of alignment struck him in a new way. It was daunting. He had a momentary vision of that unfortunate figure of Greek mythology, Sisyphus, condemned to push a huge stone up a hill, only to see it roll back down every time he got to the top. Was this going to be an exercise in futility? SEM caught the somber expression on Richard's face, and offered a measure of hope.

"Richard, aligning is a huge challenge, but it's very doable. You need to approach it systematically. That's a whole discussion we will have to save for another time. Part of the answer is in the next one—'selling.'"

With another characteristic dramatic gesture, he pounded his open palm on the word "selling" on CAS' flip chart sheet.

"Why is this important?"

"I suppose because if you don't sell the direction and the need for alignment, you're going to have a tough time implementing it."

"Exactly. It's like a politician on a campaign—you can never oversell your message. When you're getting tired of talking it up, that's when the message is starting to get through."

"I'm not much of a charismatic speaker," Richard ventured. "And I've never been a gifted communicator."

"You don't need to be a gifted communicator, just a committed one. In fact, gifted communicators can be at a disadvantage because they tend to rely on their ability to communicate rather than on the persuasiveness of a clear sense of direction and a compelling set of values."

SEM paused. He needed to shift the focus of the conversation.

"Richard, let's go back to the tension between CAS and POM. Both are absolutely necessary, but the mix changes at different levels of the company." SEM drew a rectangle with a diagonal line across it. At the top of the vertical axis he wrote "CEO" and at the bottom he wrote "FLM"— "Frontline manager," he explained. "Everything in between the two are progressive levels of leadership."

On the bottom he wrote, "Relative Time Spent with CAS or POM."

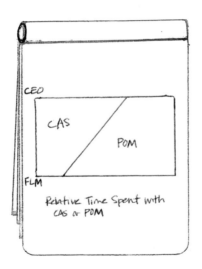

"The point is that a frontline manager will spend more time with POM and, as that leader's responsibilities increase, so the mix changes—until it's virtually flipped around when you get to the CEO. If—just for the sake of illustration—a frontline manager spends 90 percent of his or her time on POM and 10 percent on CAS, it might as well be flipped around for a CEO—90 percent on CAS and 10 percent on POM. Now let's pause a moment and think about the feedback your leadership team gave you. Where are they saying you spend most of your time?"

Richard got up and went to the flip chart. He drew a new box, but this time, with a very different diagonal line. He didn't even need to refer to the notes he'd made from their feedback.

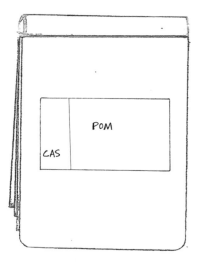

"I think that's what they'd say. It's certainly closer to my reality. Perhaps even a little too generous. Instead of working with CAS, I've had a hard time letting go of POM."

Richard understood. SEM felt like an attorney who could now rest his case. Turning to CAS and POM, he asked them, "Gentlemen, have I been fair to you?"

CAS and POM looked at each other, turned to SEM and nodded in unison.

"What about you, SEM," Richard asked, "what do your initials stand for?"

"I was going to touch on that briefly. In my focus on how leaders bring out the best in their people, I emphasize three things. The first is making sure you match their talents and strengths to the function that calls for them the most. So 'Select and Match'—that's the 'S.'" He wrote it up on the flip chart.

"But that's not enough. You can get someone in the right job for their particular set of skills and talents, but they may be clueless about the expectations you have of their performance. So you need to 'Explain and Clarify Expectations.'" SEM added that to the flip chart.

"Now, if you have done nothing but those two, you have done pretty well. In fact, you're likely to have people who are highly motivated because they are doing stuff they are good at and they know what's expected of them. But you can do better still by consciously applying principles of motivation and by making sure you are helping them strengthen their talents." SEM added "Motivate and Develop" to the flip chart.

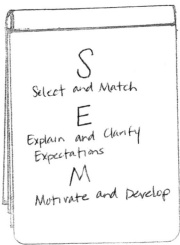

"Richard, I'm not going to go further into this because we have a special assignment for you to help you understand my focus—the people-leadership focus—but before we give it to you, let's clarify how the three of us work together—CAS, POM and I."

SEM went back to the flip chart. With strong and dramatic gestures, he draw a large rectangular cube with a diagonal line across its face.

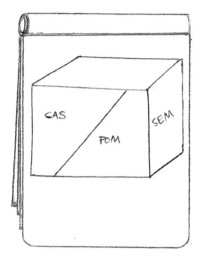

"Richard, leaders need me whatever their level of leadership. The frontline manager needs to apply what I emphasize, and so do you as a CEO—and so does everyone in between the two of you. But leaders need to apply my focus differently—and this is key—depending on the level of leadership they exercise. You and every frontline manager in the company will need to 'select and match' the right person to the job, for example, but what you as CEO will be looking for in your direct reports will be very different from what frontline managers will be looking for in theirs."

SEM paused for a moment and put his large, chubby hand across the face of the cube. "So in order to apply my three principles effectively, you have to understand the dynamic between CAS and POM—then you can apply my focus appropriately." He paused again and looked at Richard.

"Is this making sense?"

It was. Richard realized that if he were operating two or more levels below his current level of leadership responsibility, he couldn't possibly apply SEM's principles effectively. He needed to understand where the mix needed to be for his direct reports before he could select and match, explain and clarify expectations, and effectively motivate and develop them.

"Richard, we're going to stop right here, and instead of looking at me as a set of bullet points on a flip chart, I'd like you to see what it looks like when a leader listens to me. So here's the assignment I mentioned earlier. Go and find Ben Windsor who heads up the OEM division, and learn what you can from him. He's a crusty old man, but he's good. People want to work for him and people want the people who work for him."

Richard remembered Ben or, rather, hearing about him. His depart-ment consistently scored high in employee feedback reports, but Richard had never paid much attention to what he did.

At this point, CAS stood up and walked over to Richard.

"Richard, one last thing before you head off to Ben. We wanted to give you something."

CAS pulled a wooden cube out of his pocket. Somewhat ceremoniously, he handed it to Richard, and Richard took it almost with a touch of reverence. He remembered the cube he'd seen in his father's office and wondered if it was the same one. He wouldn't have been surprised if it were. But beyond the recollection of that cube in his father's office, the feeling of familiarity returned. He had seen the cube somewhere else before, but he still couldn't place it.

A Visit to the OEM
Division

It was hard to tell his age. He had a timeless quality to him; certainly not young, but certainly nowhere near decrepitude or irrelevance. Ben had been in the same job ever since Richard could remember, but despite hearing his father's unusually positive comments about Ben, Richard had never felt compelled to explore what merited such accolades. His father had nicknamed him 'Big Ben,' not because of his stature (which was unimpressive) but because of his impact. His division's performance was certainly impressive; the Original Equipment Manufacturers division (known as the OEM division) serviced some of the company's largest accounts and somehow, it had a knack for keeping them coming back. But Richard had never been particularly interested in finding out why.

When SEM had given him the assignment, Richard had decided

to visit the shop floor early before finding Ben. He wanted to get a feel from the people in Ben's division what it felt like working there and he wanted to go unannounced so that there could be no hint of putting on a show. He also realized that his mere presence might alter their behavior but, with a touch of sadness, he also concluded that since he'd never been down there, few might know who he actually was.

There was nothing visually different about the OEM division. It was neat, tidy, organized—just like most other departments in the company. If there were a difference here, he thought, it wouldn't be in what was visible. So he began looking for the intangibles and slowly he began to detect a widespread, general sense of urgency. But it wasn't a frenetic urgency; it had a quiet, purposeful, deliberate feel to it, almost a calmness to it . . . unlike many departments and, he thought, unlike the divisions he had led.

Here was a positive energy and it didn't seem contrived; it felt natural. This, it occurred to him, was as evident from what was not happening as much as from what *was* happening—he didn't see anxious conversations confronting crises, huddled groups trying to solve an insoluble dilemma, managers walking briskly around with the look of a white knight on a white horse rescuing hapless souls from a disaster beyond their competence. People seemed to know what to do; the urgency was pursued without a sense of confusion or panic.

Conversation followed observation. Richard began to ask one person after another what they appreciated about working in this division. He didn't want to ask about Ben; he wanted to see if they would talk about him unprompted. Inevitably they did and he wasn't surprised. Somehow it all came back to Ben or to his managers; interestingly, when a manager was well-spoken of, it was often attributed to Ben's influence.

Richard was more intrigued than ever to meet Ben. After two hours of observation and conversation, he made his way to Ben's office. On the way, he passed several classrooms, all in use; he made a mental note to ask Ben what they were addressing.

Richard looked at the timeless face, and now that he was in front of him, he wasn't sure quite how to begin.

"Ben, some people recommended I come and pay you a visit—they figured I could learn some things from you. I took the liberty of wandering around the plant floor before finding you and I have to say I think they're right."

Ben smiled. "Crusty" had been SEM's description, but Ben's smile was a reassuring one. "I'd be glad to, Richard. I was wondering when you'd make it down here."

So Ben had been expecting him. Richard wondered whether Ben knew his three coaches, but didn't want to risk the question.

"A good place to start, Richard, is for you to tell me what you know and what you're learning."

Richard launched into as complete a summary as he could without mentioning the decision to sell and only vaguely referring to his three mentors. He described the feedback from his team, and when he mentioned the Leadership Cube, Ben interrupted him.

"So you've been introduced to the Leadership Cube. That's good."

"So you know CAS, POM and SEM?"

"Yes—the acronyms that describe organizational leadership, operational leadership and people leadership."

Ben's cryptic response was enough to deflect further probing, but it didn't stop Richard from searching Ben's face for some clue to reveal if he knew about the three occupants of the clock tower. Ben's face remained inscrutable.

"Anyway," Richard continued, "one of my three coaches suggested you could help me with the whole notion of SEM."

"Sure, we can look at that, but before we do, let's look at a couple of ideas about the Cube—and SEM's relationship to the other two." Going to two nearby flip charts, Ben drew two cubes.

"Richard, what's the difference between these two cubes? Assume that the face with the diagonal is the same size in each case."

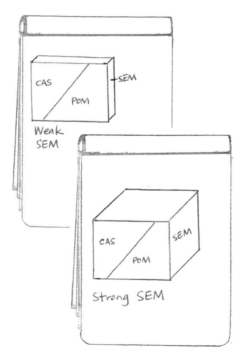

"Well, the difference is in the SEM. In the one case, it's shallow, and in the other, it's deep ... which suggests that SEM is much more fully developed in the second one."

"That's right, Richard. What's the problem with the first one?

"It doesn't have the same stability as the second one. It's more likely to topple over."

"Exactly. So you can have perfect integration and harmony between CAS and POM, but if SEM is absent, your leadership is still going to be deficient. In fact, all three have a very symbiotic relationship. With a strong SEM, but without a clear balance between CAS and POM, SEM will be far less effective because it won't be applied to the right mix of CAS and POM, and conversely, with a clear balance between CAS and POM but little or no application of SEM, CAS and POM won't have the means of taking root."

He looked at Richard. "Make sense?" Richard nodded.

"There's one other idea to learn from the Cube." Ben paused to collect his thoughts, and then continued with a question.

"Richard, what was it like adjusting to your first leadership role in the company?"

Richard described his first major assignment as a project manager, leading a group of project engineers who had previously been peers before the promotion. He had to overcome the perception of being given the job because of his last name; it had been a rough transition.

"I see that all the time," Ben responded. "Every time we bring on a new frontline manager, they invariably struggle. It's often a brutal rite of passage; we do what we can to prepare them but, in the end, you just have to live through it."

Pointing to the front face of the cube, he continued. "But in reality, the transitions further up are harder, because they are less perceptible.

As you move up, you're not necessarily aware of the changing relationship between CAS and POM. It's the frog-in-the-kettle syndrome."

Richard's puzzled expression prompted an explanation.

"You know—the frog in the kettle. Throw a frog into a pot of boiling water and it'll jump right out. But put a frog in a pot of cold water and bring it slowly to a boil . . . the frog will never jump out. It's an ugly way to die. That's what happens to leaders—just as the frog doesn't realize the temperature is changing, so leaders don't realize that the CAS/POM mix is shifting. I've seen a lot of leaders get derailed for that simple reason . . . especially in the last few years," he added. "Which is why I suppose you are here."

Ben's bluntness reminded him of CAS. In fact, the words were almost identical.

"Now, you're here to ask me about SEM. Let's talk about what that looks like. It's actually not very complicated; at least, the concept isn't. I use a simple formula: The right people in the right job with the right mandate and the right resources will release the right energy. In other words . . ." On the next sheet, he wrote out an equation with different words but the same idea.

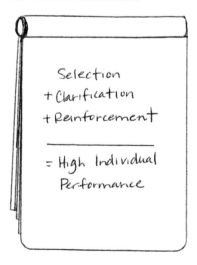

Selection
+ Clarification
+ Reinforcement
─────────────
= High Individual
Performance

"It's a different way of capturing the same idea as the acronym for SEM."

"Explain 'Selection' to me, Ben. I understand the principle, but it's not that obvious to me how you put it into practice."

"It's part science, part art. You can use resources, but you also need to rely on your gut. When it comes right down to it, there are three basic ideas for selecting someone for a job—whether your selection pool is internal or external."

He flipped over the page of the flip chart and, on a clean sheet, he drew a triangle. At the top corner, he wrote "What They Say."

"That means," Ben explained, "that you need to find out what they say about themselves in terms of their strengths and aspirations. How do they see their own strengths? Now, of course, that's not always foolproof, so you need to ask what others are saying about them."

He added "What Others Say" to the bottom right-hand corner. "That includes, by the way, instruments that assess preferences, abilities or behavioral styles. There are plenty of them out there, and at some point I can let you know which ones I use and prefer."

Writing again on the paper, he continued, "And then, of course, there's what you observe. You might uncover skills and talents that the individual isn't aware of, though, in your position, they should be coming to you with pretty high levels of self-awareness. But you'd be surprised how few senior executives have taken a serious inventory of their strengths and weaknesses."

Richard thought about the feedback from his team. That was the beginning of a pretty serious inventory.

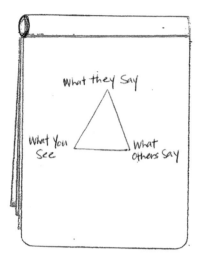

"What about 'Clarification'?" Richard asked. "What's the trick to that?"

"If you select the right person for the job but you don't make it clear what you expect from them, that person will end up doing whatever they think is best and it may be quite different from what you had in mind. It's sometimes hard for leaders to recognize how much frustration they cause by not being clear—we expect people to read our minds and then we get upset when they misread them."

"How can we be clear without micro-managing?" Richard was thinking of the feedback from his team.

"Being clear has nothing to do with micro-managing. In fact, the clearer you are in what you want to see happen, the less inclined you will be to micro-manage. Now that also means that you have to be clear not only about the end result but also about the level of performance in pursuing that result—in other words, what kind of quality you expect both in the product and the process."

"What if you are dealing with people who don't have the level of competence the assignment requires?"

"Richard, this is Delegation 101. You always delegate and assign tasks or roles with an appropriate level of instruction and facilitation; anything more is micro-managing and anything less is irresponsibility."

After that rap on the knuckles, Richard wanted to press on.

"What about 'Reinforcement'?"

"That's the 'Motivate and Develop' in SEM. Actually, the one I focus on is development. I find that if I am very consciously developing the leaders under me—assuming that I'm selecting well and being clear—they end up being pretty motivated. And I focus on their strengths: I want to see their strengths get even better. If I have a Michael Jordan on my team, I want to make sure that he's playing at his best. The temptation is to leave the Michael Jordans alone because they can do pretty well without input, but if I do that, I do them a disservice; that's a temptation I work hard at resisting."

"Do you have a plan? It sounds quite disciplined."

"It is. It's deliberate and planned. And it's tailored to the individual. But actually they are the ones who come up with it. I just provide the framework to help them figure out how they can get better. And because they come up with it, they own it."

All this was a lot to digest. Richard looked at the notes he'd been taking and realized how much he still had to learn. But he was beginning to feel as if he now had a structure to guide that learning.

When he looked up and caught Ben's intense gaze, he realized that great leadership really was a core value Ben cherished deeply. What the company needed was a lot more Bens.

Richard had found what he had come looking for, but before he left Ben, there was still one question Richard needed to ask.

"Ben, what difference does it make to you what kind of leadership I provide? I look at what I see here and everything seems to be humming along very nicely. What difference do I make to you? What difference does my leadership—good or bad—make to what you do here every day?"

"Richard, that's a very astute question. And let me answer it this way. When I compare my job under your leadership to my job under your father's leadership . . ." Ben paused, picking his words; Richard was beginning to wonder whether the question was that astute after all.

"Well, let me say that your father made it very much easier for me," Ben continued. "He made sure that the company's purpose, vision and values were pretty clear to everyone in the whole company, at least as much as he could, and that made it much easier for me to tie what goes on in this department to what the company tries to do in the marketplace."

Richard didn't interrupt him; he sensed there was more. There was.

"One of the biggest differences is that our communication and interaction with other departments was much easier. We all seemed to be whistling the same tune. Now it feels very competitive. One of the interesting measures to me is that under your father's leadership, my people who were recruited to other departments were generally positive about the move; today they don't want to leave. Those who do get transferred want to come back—and if they can't, they quit, unless it's been a down market, then they tend to stay, but they're disgruntled."

Richard realized that turnover as a symptom of malaise went much deeper than just his leadership team. For the first time, he was grateful for the down market that kept good people from leaving, but it also added to the urgency. He needed to initiate change before the market began to tick its way back.

"There's more, Richard," Ben continued. "When you as the company's leader don't give a clear trumpet call, people end up just being busy —busy work, not necessarily productive work. That in its turn has its own set of negative consequences. People get more tired doing less. Work gets duplicated and, worse still, it ends up being the wrong work. Productivity and efficiency decline. These days, for example, we find we have to wait longer for other departments to get back to us, simply because their productivity has declined. That obviously has a negative impact on us, even though we have our act together —at least compared to the other departments."

Ben paused. He wanted to reinforce the point with a point of clarification.

"Richard, CAS isn't something you just do at the top of the company. I have to do CAS as well within the OEM division."

He flipped over the sheet to the next clean sheet and drew a now-familiar diagram. But he made a significant change to it. He added "OEM division" to the top, crossed out "CEO" and added "Ben."

"You see, Richard, just as you have to think about the company in the bigger context of the marketplace and the industry, I also have to think about the OEM division in its bigger context—which happens to be the rest of the company. I have to set and shape the direction of the division so that it has the greatest level of relevance and contribution to the company as a whole. I need to align the division around that direction, and I need to constantly sell to everyone working in it." As Ben continued, the intensity in his voice raised a notch.

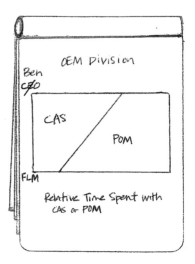

"The point is this. If you're not doing *your* job with CAS, I can't do *my* job with CAS—nor can any of the other division heads, because there's too much confusion in the greater context we operate in—internally throughout the company."

Ben paused and gave Richard a focused look. "So, to answer your question, Richard: Yes, your leadership has a huge impact on my effectiveness as a leader. However good I may be."

The two hours he'd spent with Ben seemed like ten minutes, perhaps the most deeply thought-provoking ten minutes he could remember spending. He thanked Ben warmly and, as Richard was heading out the door, Ben offered him a final word of comfort.

"If it's any encouragement, Richard, your father also paid me a visit, a long time ago. He had to learn this too."

Richard looked at him. How old was he really?

Slowly, pensively, Richard retraced his steps back to his office. 'Big

Ben' had indeed made an impact on him. And then it struck him: Big Ben was also a clock tower, a timeless timekeeper in London.

As he came back into the central courtyard, Richard happened to glance up at the clock tower. Funny that he'd never seen it, but there it was—a shield as a coat of arms, and in the middle was a faded but still clearly visible cube, with a diagonal line across the front face of the cube. That's where he'd seen it.

The Confession

"Listen. I need to level with you."

The sudden stillness in the room caught Richard by surprise and he looked down nervously at the table.

With a deep breath, he looked at his leadership team and continued.

"These past three months have been the most significant time in my career. I've been learning things about myself and my leadership that have been profoundly uncomfortable. I've realized how one-dimensional my leadership has been and, if it had been the right dimension, that would have been somewhat redemptive, but," as he thought about his operational obsession, "it's been the wrong dimension for the kind of leadership I should have been giving, and there's been nothing redemptive about my leadership. Which compels me to thank you for the patience you have demonstrated."

He caught a glimpse of the clock tower out of the corner of his eye, and he thought he could see the warm glow of the lamps in the upper chambers. It was a reassuring sight.

"I've learned a great deal about leadership." If ever there were an understatement, he thought, that was it.

"And I have also learned that the most significant thing about an organization is what goes on in the minds of its leaders." As it rolled off his tongue, he realized that he believed it. Even though he had borrowed it, now he owned it.

With some gusto and a surprising level of conviction, he launched into an explanation of the Leadership Cube. Fueled by incisive questions, his explanation went on much longer than he intended and, with an effort, he reined in the discussion. "There is something else I need to tell you." Trust had been growing between Richard and his team, so this change of direction wasn't met with quite the same uncertainty as before, but it was said with enough firmness for them to focus intently on what Richard was going to say next.

"The board reached the decision to sell."

The stunned silence told Richard that no one had leaked the information. Before they could voice their reaction, Richard continued.

"Now, I believe we can change that decision. But I need your help."

The War Room

It wasn't long before the barrage of questions came.

"When did they decide to sell?" A little over two months ago.

"Why did they decide to sell?" That was harder to answer. Richard opted for honesty.

"It has to do with my leadership." He explained his own short-comings, and used them to reaffirm the deeply held corporate value of great leadership that he himself had ignored for so long. He mentioned his three mentors, but he was glad no one probed. They wouldn't have believed him anyway.

Ever ready with the right question, Kathy was the first to respond to his explanation. "What's it going to take to change the board's mind?"

"Good question. I think they need to be convinced about three things. First, they need to know that I'm exercising the right type of leadership—effectively living out and teaching the Leadership Cube. Second, they need to be convinced we are thinking strategically—that we have a clear vision, that we have a strategy to get us there, and that we know the current markets and are anticipating future markets as best we can. And third, they need to be convinced that we are proactively developing leaders throughout the company. They'll want to know that we are developing the leaders we need to get us to the vision we are pursuing."

Silence followed. It wasn't that long, but it was long enough for Richard to wonder who would be the first to turn in his resignation and how quickly the others would follow. He wasn't expecting what happened next.

"We need a plan."

Kathy's statement, addressed to all in the room, unleashed a torrent of pent-up energy and creativity he never knew this group possessed. Idea after idea poured out, and before long, people were taking turns at the flip chart to capture them.

Finally someone said, "We need more than a plan—we need a war room."

The idea came from Bill, his CFO, not one Richard would have pictured as particularly combative.

"Look," Bill elaborated, "we don't have long to turn this baby around —we have just over six months to conduct this campaign and we need some kind of command central where we can regroup and direct this campaign."

The idea caught on. Richard proposed the conference room between his office and Jane's work area. It had the advantage of being discreetly accessible. Jane would need to be brought in on the conspiracy.

Without wasting any time, the meeting adjourned to the newly designated war room. The discussion surged on; options were explored and assignments were distributed. Among them was Bill's assignment to investigate IQ^2 and a heated discussion revolved around its value as an acquisition. Every one of Richard's three conditions for board acceptance was addressed and, in each case, responsibilities were clearly assigned and defined. Groups formed and reformed, and flip chart sheets repapered the wall.

The energy in the room underscored the full scope of the challenge they faced. No one was blind to it. Richard thought of that old country song about a rookie truck driver lamenting that if he had 40 acres, he "could turn this rig around." They didn't have 40 acres to turn this rig around.

Somber though the thought, Richard also observed the scene with a deep sense of gratitude and not without a measure of healthy humility—something he had never experienced before. Even if the company did end up being sold, he now knew he had a different benchmark for success. His role was to help these people succeed, whether they ended up here or somewhere else. Helping them make their greatest contribution was a thought that had never been so captivating.

He slipped out briefly to retrieve a brick from a pile in the parking lot and, as the meeting wound down, he passed it around for everyone to sign.

"We're rebuilding this company. I can't think of a finer group of people with whom to rebuild it."

The Coat of Arms

The sessions that followed had the look and feel at times of wartime generals second-guessing their opponent's move; at others, like staffers heatedly discussing their candidate's campaign; and at others, like a group of entrepreneurs concocting the next Microsoft™ around the kitchen table. There were highs and lows, but the momentum was gathering.

During a lull in one of these sessions, Bill was standing at the window, looking in the general direction of the clock tower.

"Hey—look at that! I've never noticed that before."

And turning to Richard, he asked, "Did you put that coat of arms up there?"

Richard looked over and saw the coat of arms with the cube in the middle—but now, it was bright, clean and stood out from the rest of the masonry as if someone had taken some bleach to clean it and a chisel to define it. He thought of his still-frequent but discreet visits to the chambers, started to shake his head, then stopped.

He looked over at Bill, smiled and nodded.

At least he'd had a part in it.

The Board Room

" S o that's it, then."

The statement was anything but the flat, empty, resigned statement of nine months ago.

The chairman looked out the window to the clock tower, though this time, it was not to avoid eye contact with the rest of the board members gathered around the table. After nine months, the company had experienced something of a rebirth. And yet, somehow, he sensed that the work of the clock tower was still incomplete. But Richard—a very different Richard—had been very persuasive and the board had bought in.

"So that's it, then. We acquire."

Afterword

Some Lessons from Richard

"Some men are born great," Shakespeare tells us, "some achieve greatness, and some have greatness thrust upon them."

Shakespeare was right—we can achieve greatness, but we need the right framework to know how to achieve it. That's what the story of Richard is about—having a framework that sets him in the direction of greatness.

A number of years ago, my wife and children gave me six tennis lessons as a Father's Day gift. I had been a recreational tennis player for most of my life, competent enough not to embarrass myself or those with whom I played, but conscious of inadequacies I didn't know how to put right. At times I voiced the need to have some lessons, and this Father's Day gift was, no doubt, intended to silence my musings.

The lessons were eye-opening. I learned very quickly that the power and accuracy of the return came not from the strength of my arm—an assumption I had labored under for years—but from the power of my legs, as I straightened my flexed knees to bring the full weight of my body into a swing that started knee-high rather than waist-high or shoulder-high. The result was a force and accuracy that surprised me as much as the unsuspecting ball that up to that point usually got the better of me. That wasn't all I learned—I learned, for example, about the value of a two-handed backhand and how to cross the court to better position myself for the next shot.

The transformation was not enough to launch me into a new career, but it did give me the knowledge I needed to improve my game, which would otherwise have limped along with no visible progress. It gave me the framework I needed to know how to improve, and I now knew how to practice well—practice without that knowledge would simply have reinforced my bad habits and my mistaken assumptions. As someone said, it isn't practice that makes perfect, only perfect practice. I now had a framework to not only play better, but also to practice well.

So it is with leadership, and so it was for Richard. Richard was very gifted, but when it came to leadership, he didn't have the right knowledge to exercise the type of leadership his responsibilities required. Much of the confusion in leadership is over the three dimensions of leadership—organizational leadership, operational leadership and people leadership—and Richard was no exception. But with the right framework, his leadership was transformed. That's what his three mentors provided him, that's what saved the company and that's what saved his career.

And that's what I hope it will do for you—take your leadership to new heights. This is not a formula with three, five, seven or ten steps.

Instead, it's a way of thinking about leadership, a conceptual framework to guide your actions as a leader.

Such a framework can strengthen and enrich your leadership because it will be fed with the right knowledge. You will know what mix of the three dimensions is most appropriate for your current leadership role and what kind of mix you will need for the roles you aspire to.

Such a framework will also help you develop and strengthen your own set of convictions about leadership. You will not only understand leadership, you will also understand organizations and how they work—especially your own. You will learn an approach that can be applied to any corporate environment.

Most important of all, such a framework will help you shape and direct your own personal growth and learning. You will know what books to read and what resources to look for.

It's difficult to overestimate the power of such a framework. Leaders stand or fall not so much by their talent or lack of it, but by their understanding or misunderstanding of what great leadership is. The aspiration of this story is to give you a better understanding of how to apply the three dimensions of leadership to your particular leadership responsibilities and a better understanding of what great leadership looks like so that you can embrace and exercise it—to help you achieve greatness, as Shakespeare put it.

A final word: Richard's story is about competence, and competence in leadership (the ability to apply the right mix of organizational, operational and people leadership to any given leadership role) is not the only ingredient in great leadership. Great leadership is also about character . . . that inner quality of moral fortitude that helps a leader choose integrity over expediency, commitment over comfort, and self-sacrifice over self-interest. Without character, competence gives us at worst well-organized crime and inhumanity, and at best sterile organizations with no soul. With Richard, it was not his character as a leader that was at issue; it was his competence as a leader.

Competence is one wing of the aircraft—character is the other, which makes character every bit as important to great leadership as competence. But more of that another time—that's the subject of another story.

Acknowledgements

While Richard and his three mentors are the product of my own musings, my thinking and writing have been greatly stimulated and enriched by some I have never met, but whose contribution I greatly respect. I have a deep appreciation for the research conducted by people such as John Kotter, Jim Collins and Jerry Porras, as well as the Gallup Group and many others. I owe them much, and they may well recognize some of their own traits in the faces of the three inhabitants of the clock tower.

Others have not only influenced me, but have also stretched me— the colleagues, clients and friends who have pushed and challenged my thinking and practice, and in so doing, have strengthened and refined them. Dave Cornett, Greg Dawson, Bruce Jamieson and Greg Wiens as partners became not only highly respected colleagues but deeply valued friends, as have others who walk the same path with me as colleagues and clients—all committed to exercising and teaching great leadership. I owe them much and enjoy them greatly.

Betsy, my wife, deserves special praise. Her support and feedback have been a powerful encouragement, and the impact of her presence and companionship in the experiences that eventually brought life to Richard and his three mentors is incalculable. Eric Bell at The Gordian Publishing House masterfully managed this publication with an admirable blend of patience and persistence, and Brynley Weigle brought her creativity in abundance. And finally, as a man of faith, I would be remiss not to acknowledge my indebtedness to the One whose embodiment of great leadership I only dimly reflect, but nonetheless aspire to live and teach.

About the Author

Antony Bell is the president and CEO of Leader Development Inc., a leadership and organization development firm whose purpose is to provide the framework and relationships that enable leaders to understand, exercise and teach great leadership. Its leadership development specialists come with extensive leadership experience and strong academic credentials, and include former CEOs and senior corporate executives, PhDs, psychologists and senior military officers. The company is recognized for its ability to help organizations engage in significant change, for the effectiveness of its executive team development and for the quality of its executive coaching.

Antony Bell grew up in Australia, France and Great Britain, and his professional and executive experience covers the UK, France, Germany, Switzerland, Holland, South Africa, and the US. He earned his bachelor's degree in business and economics in the UK, and his master's in European law and business institutions in France. Over the years, he has worked with hundreds of professional leaders—all looking for a path to greatness in leadership. He is a regular contributor to business magazines and journals, and he is the author of *Great Leadership*.

He and his wife Betsy currently make their home in Columbia, South Carolina.

For more information on LeaderDevelopment Inc.
or on Antony Bell as a speaker, please visit
www.leaderdevelopmentinc.com or call 803-748-1005.

If you have enjoyed The Clock Tower,
you will want to read Great Leadership.

Published by Davies-Black
2006

*This powerful, innovative overview of great leadership provides a com-
plete and thorough framework that leaders and would-be leaders
can use, whatever the kind of leadership they exercise, and in whatever context they exercise it. It presents all the critical components
of leadership in a coherent model that unifies all of the fragmented
viewpoints, theories, concepts and notions about leadership—each
of which is part of the story—into one easy-to-grasp, consolidated,
workable paradigm.*

Great Leadership *provides more depth and detail on the functions
of organizational leadership, operational leadership and people leadership than you encountered in* The Clock Tower, *and it also de-
velops character as a key ingredient of great leadership. It presents
this framework in a way that is not only conceptually sound, but also
intensely usable.* Great Leadership *gives leaders real answers in
their quest for real leadership.*

Praise for *Great Leadership*

"*Great Leadership really makes sense of what great leadership looks like. It combines profound insight with a very practical and usable framework to exercise great leadership and, in doing so, it fills a void in the literature on leadership. Corporate leaders—at all levels—should read and assimilate it. I highly recommend this wonderful book.*"

The Honorable Jack Kemp, former Congressman, Cabinet Secretary, and Vice-Presidential candidate; business consultant, corporate board member, syndicated columnist, member of non-profit and university boards, former NFL quarterback for 13 years.

"*This is a great book for people who want to give serious thought to the application of great leadership. It is for those who are looking for more than superficial answers and who are willing to embrace the importance of both character and competence—the two themes around which the book is structured. This is an erudite work and reads very well.*"

John A. Kaneb, Chairman Gulf Oil Company, President of Catamount Companies, partner in the World Champion Boston Red Sox baseball franchise, Trustee, University of Notre Dame.

"*Great Leadership is a must-read for professionals from all sectors. It dissects the art of leadership into the critical elements of competence and character. The use of dynamic examples and easily understood models brings this oftentimes complex subject to life. This is a great primer for junior and senior leaders alike and easily converted into a meaningful and purposeful development program.*"

Lieutenant General Lawson W. Magruder III (Retired U.S. Army), commanding general of three major organizations, including the historic 10th Mountain Division. He has led soldiers in combat, on domestic disaster relief missions and peace operations worldwide, and is recognized as one of the key trainers who contributed to the rebuilding of the Army after the Vietnam War. Awarded the Distinguished Service Medal (highest peacetime award in the military).

Currently serves as Executive Director for the Institute for the Protection of American Communities at the University of Texas.

"A must-read for anyone even remotely interested in leadership today."

Al Walker, business consultant, author of "Thinking Big and Living Large," past-president of the National Speakers' Association.

"This excellent look at leadership from a global and historical perspective meets current needs of leaders in a way I have not seen anywhere else. It fills an important void in the deluge of leadership literature by providing practical, innovative direction for both novice and expert leaders. The stories of great leaders are inspiring, challenging today's CEOs to rise above mediocrity."

Dr. Kathy R. Hopkins, CEO, The National Institute for Learning Disabilities

"This book lays the foundation for great leadership and allows developing leaders to be exposed to the key elements of great leadership. It shows that with the right framework, ordinary people can become influential leaders and, in this sense, it demonstrates that leaders are made, not born. People who start with this solid base are on their way to becoming great leaders."

Reid Dove, CEO, AAA Cooper Transportation

"Tony Bell has managed to craft a very readable and focused treatise on the essentials of leadership. I have had the pleasure of working with Tony and seen him translate many of the concepts in this book for management audiences across this country. Great Leadership very effectively makes the case for the critical role of character and competence in the making of great leaders. Simply put, his proposition

is that leadership is a source of competitive advantage. Its exercise requires individuals and institutions to address the issue of character first which is both an introspective and environmental data-gathering exercise so that before leadership is practiced as an art, the leader is grounded with a full appreciation of his/her character advantages or shortcomings. It suggests a methodology to enhance "followership" by expanding the capacity or competence of the leader to embrace the full responsibility that comes with the gift of leadership.

Most business leaders who are not educated in the development of leadership competencies most often rely on what Tony identifies as intuition or experience to guide their decision making. Correctly, he suggests that neither of these options gives you sufficient insight necessary to make the best choices and continues to confuse business leaders to the truth of leadership. Leadership is not situational, although its practice requires situational flexibility. Leadership is grounded in the truth of human relationships and what was effectively practiced 2000 years ago is just as effective today. The advantage we have today is that teachers such as Tony have distilled the accumulated wisdom of our culture on the subject of great leadership so that we can learn as we practice and make the necessary adjustments along the way to avoid the very human tragedies that invariably happen when leadership fails."

Michael P. Kane, Senior Vice President, Holcim (US)

Available at all retail and online bookstores, or call Davies-Black Publishing at 800-624-1765, or order online at www.davies-black.com.

Also available from LeaderDevelopment Inc. at 803-748-1005 or www.leaderdevelopmentinc.com.